DAVID SEIDNER

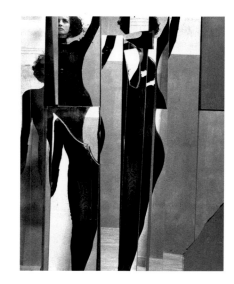

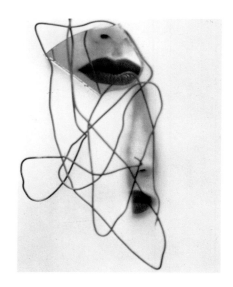
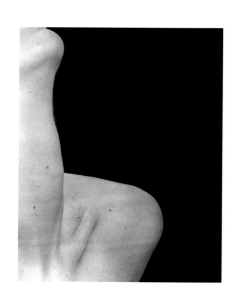

DAVID SEIDNER

WITH A TEXT BY
PATRICK MAURIÈS

Rizzoli
NEW YORK

FIRST PUBLISHED IN THE UNITED STATES OF AMERICA IN 1989
BY RIZZOLI INTERNATIONAL PUBLICATIONS, INC.
300 PARK AVENUE SOUTH, NEW YORK, NY 10010
ALL RIGHTS RESERVED. NO PART OF THIS PUBLICATION
MAY BE REPRODUCED IN ANY MANNER WHATSOEVER
WITHOUT PERMISSION IN WRITING BY
RIZZOLI INTERNATIONAL PUBLICATIONS, INC.
CONCEIVED AND DESIGNED BY DAVID SEIDNER
TRANSLATED FROM THE FRENCH BY DAVID BRITT
PRINTED AND BOUND IN WEST GERMANY

COPYRIGHT © 1989 SCHIRMER/MOSEL VERLAG GMBH, MUNICH

ISBN · 0-8478-1114-X · LC · 89 · 42807

ACKNOWLEDGMENTS

I ESPECIALLY WISH TO THANK SAMIA SAOUMA FOR HER INVALUABLE SUPPORT, ENCOURAGEMENT AND FRIENDSHIP. SPECIAL THANKS ALSO TO PIERRE BERGÉ. I WOULD ALSO LIKE TO EXPRESS MY GRATITUDE TO THE FOLLOWING FOR THEIR COLLABORATION: AZZEDINE ALAÏA, BRIGITTE REISS-ANDERSEN, JOSE LUIS ARMIJO, MARC BALET, NICHOLAS BOREL, HAMISH BOWLES, EVE BRENNAN, DEBORAH BROOME, GABRIELLE BUCHAERT, MADELEINE COFANO, DANIEL FRENNA, NADINE GASC, PAMELA GEIGER, PAUL GOBEL, DIDIER GRUMBACH, YVES HABBAS, ICONOLAB, FRANÇOIS JOVER, MARYLOU LUTHER, PHOPHIE MATHIAS, PATRICK MAURIÈS, FABIAN MIMOUNI, RENATE GALLOIS-MONTBRUN, FLORENCE MÜLLER, YVES OPPENHEIM, MANUELA PAVESI, PATTI PODESTA, CLARA SAINT, YVES SAINT LAURENT, NELSON SEPULVEDA, BETSY SUSSLER, GABRIELLE TANA, GREY ZISSER AND, OF COURSE, ALL THOSE WHO APPEAR IN THE PHOTOGRAPHS. I WOULD ALSO LIKE TO THANK THE FOLLOWING MAGAZINES FOR THEIR COOPERATION: BOMB MAGAZINE, NEW YORK; CONDÉ NAST S.A., PARIS; EDIZIONI CONDÉ NAST S.P.A., MILAN; HARPER'S & QUEEN, LONDON; INTERVIEW MAGAZINE, NEW YORK; JARDINS DES MODES, PARIS. THE BLACK AND WHITE PRINTS IN THIS BOOK WERE MADE BY PATRICK WELLEM AND CAROLINE DARTOIS AT CENTRAL COLOR, PARIS. TYPOGRAPHY BY THOMAS ELSNER.

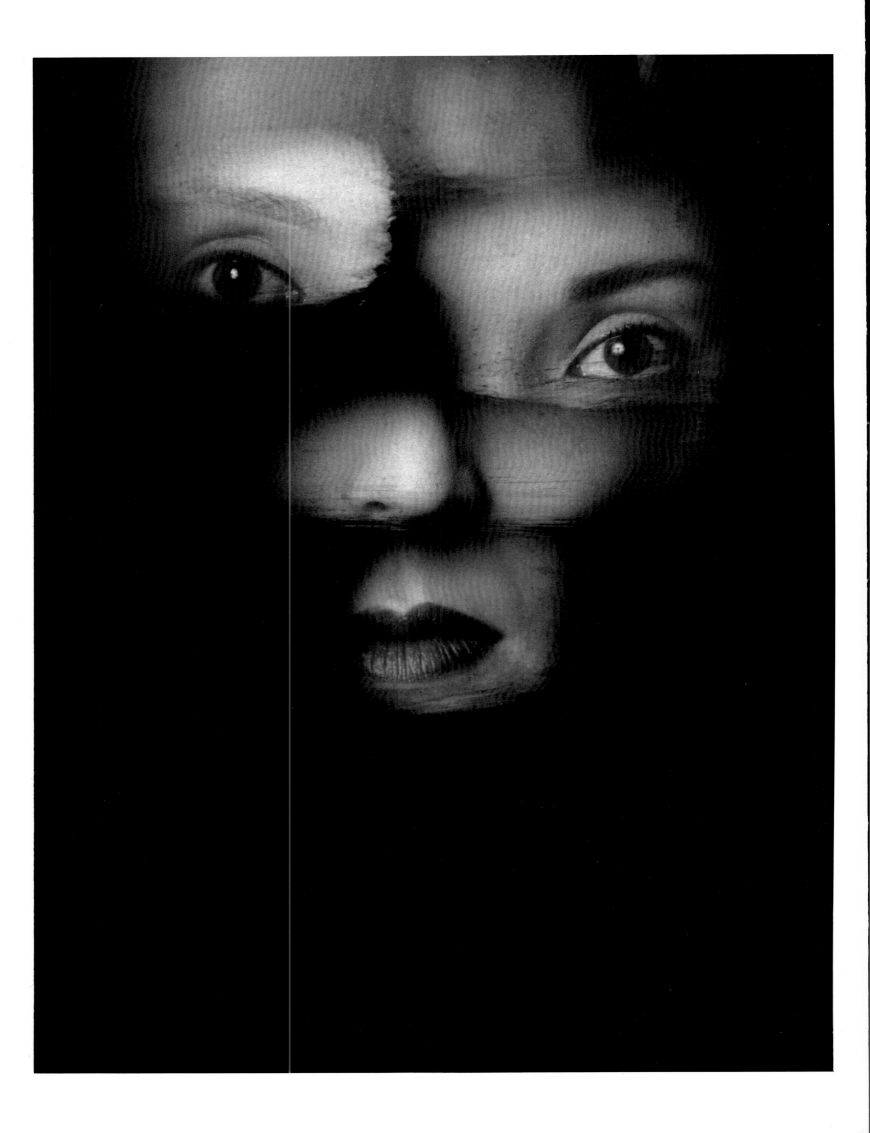

PATRICK MAURIÈS
FRAGMENTS ON FRAGMENTS

1. Dismemberment is not uncommon among the gods. Osiris, torn to bits by his jealous, evil, jackal-headed brother Set, and cast into the Nile, was resurrected by Isis with the help of Nephthys and Anubis who put him back together piece by piece. And Dionysos, born of the union between a mortal and Zeus, suffered Hera's jealousy, while his foster mother, surrounded by frenzied Bacchantes, ripped her other child apart . . . , the infant Dionysos a victim of the resentful Lycurgus who was himself torn limb from limb after cutting his own son to pieces.

Myths, clouded in our memories, themselves frayed and tattered by time, of which we manage to retain only a few images – those bleeding bodies, twitching convulsively in the moonlight – evoke unquestionably, I think, the photography, the vision, of David Seidner. Founded on grief, yet open to the hope of return and regeneration. There is one photograph in particular, of a young man, that has a unique position in Seidner's work: the youth's slender, outstretched form, his luminous beauty, is marked by a patch of blinding whiteness at the groin (69). Of the fourteen fragments into which Osiris' body was torn, Isis found all except one: the phallus, which had been swallowed, according to legend, by the fish called oxyrhynchus.

2. The phallus, symbolic organ, whose absence and introjection are, as we know, the basis of the entire symbolic system of psychoanalysis. Until the phallus is 'lost', or eliminated, no meaning can circulate, and no relation to the Other can be possible. Subject also of misunderstanding and misconception, vehicle for perversion: thus, in fetishism, the adored object, the source of gratification, is said to refer to the imagined phallus of the mother. And the mechanics of fetishism might well serve as a basis for a first reading, however simplistic, of these images by David Seidner. With regard to the fashion photographs, they blow up, distend, magnify, overexpose the softness of satin, the shimmer of tulle, the sheen of velvet, the opulence of damask, the flow of silks; they caress a hipline, a rounded muscle, the sheathing of a leg, the plunge of a neckline or the bend of a wrist. The skin lives with the fabric, the texture made rich by the contrast of a crumbling decor. Fetishistic also is the way in which the subject is obsessively scrutinized, outlined and dissected, isolated like a separate entity, a free-floating object, some fragment of a body or face, a torso or a piece of clothing – caught in one fleeting, impossible instant.

3. No doubt some future historian of the mind will say that fragmentation, both literal and philosophical, is one of the great ideological themes – if not the central theme – of present-day culture. It is a motif inherited from German Romanticism; it springs also from our acute awareness of the impossibility of aspiring to a total image of anything, and from our rejection of academic exposition: that rigid form which, in literary terms, Roland Barthes classified as dissertation, and which is an attempt to espouse the rhythm of thought, to reflect the true order of things. The right to be fragmentary is now asserted in philosophy as it is in literature, in the humanities as it is in music. It will also be recognized as one of the great *topoi* of modernist painting, which treats incompletion as essential to any accurate and faithful rendering of experience in all its mobility, its partiality, its speed, and its fallibility. Strange vision, like that of an insect's compound eye, with its myriad details juxtaposed but separate; a reinterpretation of the analytical vision of Cubism, shunning

unitary perspective, evoking the constant shifts of focus, the readjustments inherent to vision, and the flow and varying intensity of light.

The universality of this theme – its potential as a commonplace of contemporary culture – tends to blur its definition, to undermine its nature and its inevitability, and to cushion its disruptive force. Seidner's photography – in its own evolutionary terms – must be seen as a part of this complex, with all that it entails: all that the dissociative sensibility leaves unstated but forcefully conveys.

4. Paradoxically, the absence of wholeness in Seidner's work makes one feel as if this severed vision of reality were normal. Filling in the blanks becomes a natural, invisible process. It gives one the pleasure of defining, reconstructing, even sculpting what emerges only on the contours of the photographs. The fluting of the charioteer's tunic, shifted to the edge of the image (27); the corolla of a diaphanous skirt, sliding out of frame (15); a face in lost profile, showing the bone-structure, the sinuosities of cheek and neck (4); in the concentric circles which mark our approach, the art of framing, the concern with composition is what we see first. But here the very act of composing – with all its traditional implications of centring, controlling, confining, calculating – actually opens up the image, shifts its centre of gravity, renders it unstable.

In all this, Seidner is placing himself within a tradition that includes not only the *Japonisme* of the late nineteenth century, as represented by Degas and Lautrec, but also the cinematography of Orson Welles and the work of the great graphic artists of the 1950s: the masters of ellipsis and asymmetry, of unstable forms and formal openness, and the exemplars of 'anticlassicism', as defined (somewhat over-systematically) by the Viennese art historians of the 1920s.

What might be regarded as Seidner's formalism – the extreme refinement of his compositions, his fondness for a linear, calligraphic definition of the body – is in reality a kind of wilful vertigo. Nothing illustrates this better than his manner of working. Long exposures, allowing the body to show itself, to unfold in its own time, to fall into its own rhythm, its own elegance. He takes his time; not, as one might imagine, in order to establish a total, premeditated control, but in order to take his subject unawares. Captured at the critical moment, the subject discovers an identity and escapes from the dead weight of preparation, the (necessary) outer paraphernalia of technique. This is what the Greek Sophists called *Kairos*, the right moment. There is a striking instance of it in that incredible fashion photograph in which the sharp clarity of the profile and the ineffable elegance of the taut arms, stretched out to catch at some fugitive reality, are seen not so much against the black velvet background as against the blurred rustle, the flight – so slow in the lens's eye, and yet so sudden, so impalpable – of an acid-green silk dress (15).

5. A certain languor in suddenness. A rendering of *sprezzatura* – the studied nonchalance that Italians in the sixteenth century regarded as the essence of physical grace and formal sensibility – this phrase might serve as a good definition of elegance: another basic quality of Seidner's work, and one that tends to lend itself to misinterpretation and controversy. Elegance is the quality that Kleist, in his essay on the marionette theatre, referred to as grace: the body's ability to coincide with its own centre of gravity. The essential

characteristic of grace is that it gives us the illusion of escaping, even if only for an instant, from the grip of time; and yet it is embodied in forms which are codified and remain the prisoners of history. Thus, beyond the immediate, 'present' elegance of Seidner's subjects, we sense, faint as a watermark, the shadow of the elegant models of the 1950s, with all the associations that they bring with them: associations that are personal to everyone yet are destined, within a generation or two, to vanish. And yet there is no nostalgia here, nothing pointed, nothing definite: there is only a dim reminiscence, a fondness for a certain morphology – with its elongated necks, its acerbic profiles, and its unencumbered, updrawn line – which is rendered all the more poignant by the force of allusion.

6. All of which brings us to the fact that David Seidner is also – or equally – a fashion photographer: a term notoriously misunderstood and misjudged. Like fashion drawing, and indeed like the culture of fashion in general, fashion photography is fertile ground for misconception, moralizing, and all manner of spurious value judgments. Like them, it reflects (and is contaminated by) the frivolity of the milieu and of the object shown, by the body's narcissism, and by an absence of 'thought' and profundity. Or such, at least, tends to be the view of those who, although quite 'enlightened' enough to reject (and rightly so) the false opposition between Form and Content, nevertheless persist in contrasting photography proper with fashion photography. They fail to see that by so doing they are treating 'fashion' as a Content, a Thing Signified, sufficient in itself to disqualify the image from any consideration in terms of internal arrangement, intrinsic logic, rules, tradition, history. It is as if it were necessary to distance oneself from fashion and its pleasures by paying one's dues, as it were, to a deceptively virulent form of Modernist puritanism.

The fact is that Seidner's photography belongs from every point of view – including that of generalization and prejudice – to the tradition of the grand formal portrait which can be traced back, long before the golden age of fashion photography (Avedon, Penn, Horst, Blumenfeld, Beaton, Hoyningen-Huene), to the society painting of the turn of the century (from Sargent to Boldini, taking in Laszlo and Jacques-Emile Blanche), and further still, to the court painting exemplified with such death-laden brilliance by the Florentine Mannerists.

That static, anti-natural quality found in Mannerism is echoed by a kind of inorganic representation of the body in Seidner's work, revealed through artifice, exaggerated and rendered natural. This distortion of reality is memorably embodied in the extraordinary triptych in which the shadowed, elongated eye of the model is stunningly, elliptically, improbably, and yet 'really', juxtaposed with her spine (1). The immaterial 'mirror of the soul' faces the weight of matter, the mineral substance of a structure; the body, rapturously defying all expectations, is an icon of hyperbole. The living body becomes a landscape, hollowed and valleyed; swellings emboss the pure outline of an outstretched neck. They irresistibly recall the notorious additional vertebrae of Ingres' *Grande Odalisque*, which so offended his traditionalist critics: the very stigmata of art.

7. A certain critical orthodoxy would prompt one to weigh the noble aspect (that is to say, personal versus commissioned) of Seidner's work, against the base (commercial photography, a predilection for finery,

and the exaltation of the meaningless). Portraiture and fashion photography might indeed be noble pursuits if there were no demand and no commissions. Seidner's commissioned work requires no apology. It conveys a deep-seated sense of the theatrical, the construction of artifice.

Many of these portraits are the result of a curious process that eludes the untutored eye of the beholder. They are mostly shot from above, the parodistic distortion corrected (or masked?) by a telephoto lens. This unexpected relationship of above to underneath (or the opposite, or sideways, or obliquely) catches the subject off-guard, completely altering the conventional frontal relationship of the subject to the artist, and the classical representation of the portrait. Surrounded by black, these faces have undergone an unseen operation; severed from the rest of the body, they no longer convey that familiarity we take for granted. Even the outward shape is changed and the spectator cannot place them in terms of an attitude, a gesture, a posture, or a mode of speech. Troubled by an eternally unanswered question, caught in a distant echo of the child's relationship with its mother, the face, isolated, becomes pure volume expressed by light.

8. The process, the technique, may on the other hand be totally visible, with multiple exposures which magnify and reduplicate the manipulation that has taken place, blurring the definitions of objects and beings alike. Superimpositions, in Seidner's work, recall the mythical through a kind of malfunction: they are curiosities, almost discarded relics, fated to become more and more alien to us, remnants of an outworn, almost antediluvian technology. They represent a rapid, cursory record of successive states of the same face; faithfully, they reproduce the way that memory has of dealing with irreconcilable realities, not by selecting, or contrasting, or alternating them, but rather by keeping them within a single space or on a single imponderable plane. A shorthand of memory, faithfully reproducing the imprecision of movement, the ambiguity of the real.

Paradoxical by nature, superimposition simultaneously conveys the sensation of volume and of its opposite. It 'translates' volume into a surface film, a layer without thickness, undermining it from within, so that it is dematerialized, or rather made hallucinatory. Throughout Seidner's work, volume is subject to a succession of dislocations, a series of transpositions, which violate the solidity of the body. Shadow becomes substance; the void opens to reveal the solid; positive becomes negative – as in the famous allegory of the origin of painting, in which a girl is left with nothing of her lost beloved but his shadow, more real than the real, whose outline she has traced on a wall.

9. I have already mentioned the constant preoccupation with capturing the mobility, the essential instability, of visual and experiential truth; but another theme (or the same one, from another angle) emerges when we look, for example, at the sequence of four half-faces in which the eye, purified, is seen with unbearable clarity, looking up or down, left or right, making a rhythmic succession of blinks (60/61): how better to convey the essential asymmetry of something that seems to us, by definition, smooth and perfect, harmonious to the point of banality?

These (fractured) images trap us in a weird mirage in which the world can only be seen askance. Unease is chronic and incurable: as in the virtual and probable reality of a face which disintegrates like the pattern in a kaleidoscope, just at the moment when we think we have succeeded in reconstructing it.

The same goes for those portraits by Seidner that are segmented into instalments, or rather dislocated into a succession of contiguous elements which do *not* make a whole: imperceptibly dislocated, subjected to varying focal lengths and varying degrees of graininess and definition. We are left with an uneasy, precarious apprehension of the relationships that unite the various parts of the face, the 'oval' that we take so much for granted until we are confronted — as we are here — by the demonstration that its only real attribute is that it does not exist: it is a mathematical mean, among thousands of extremes, a frozen spectre, an impossible idea.

10. Seidner speaks of the 'historical' origin of his compositions. Arriving one day to interview his own intellectual mentor, John Cage, for the *Los Angeles Times*, and having nothing with him but a telephoto lens, he was unable to take a full-length portrait; so he took five separate shots and combined them afterwards. This fascinating image of the effect of chance on the master of chance, the composer of an emblematic 'symphony of changes', brings us to the starting point of Seidner's work, which lies in the realm of sculpture, the complex dialectic of created form and change.

Nowhere, perhaps, is Seidner's concentration on the interplay of volumes and bodies in space more vital than in those miniatures in which a head is seen floating, object-like, against the darkness. There is an abrupt clash here with what is 'naturally' expected of photography, which is its capacity to go beyond the powers of sight, to provide a revelation through the grace of technology, to augment visibility, and thus to 'enlarge'. These images, on the contrary, are condensed, packed tight with energy; they do not set out to develop or unfold surfaces, but to place them within a sequence, a rhythm (analogous to that which informs the entire construction of the present work), a relationship with the Other, with whiteness, with shadow, and with whatever lies in between.

11. Other photographs of Seidner's — great black plates with surfaces scratched or rubbed away to reveal fractions of a face — more naturally recall painting, the sensuous action of covering a surface, cancelling out by overexposing, or revealing by scraping. Others again — sumptuous, ghostly costumes which clothe the absence of a body, standing out against crudely daubed backgrounds in light colours — are direct appeals to whatever joyous sense of theatre we ourselves may possess. This same dimension always remains subtly present in Seidner's pictures: in the staging, sotto-voce — or more simply in the placing in space within an interplay of diagonals and intersections — and also in his obvious fondness for certain materials, especially plaster. A material that is rich and yet tonally neutral, solid and yet fragile; which can renew itself, take on colour, or wear away; which testifies to the passage of time and instantly reminds us of the short-lived splendour of a stage set, the very stuff of illusion.

In the photographs taken for the Musée de la Mode, in Paris, the whole world becomes backstage, an accumulation of assorted objects — fragments of sets; plaster casts; lost, broken, dusty props — suddenly seen beneath a cold, clear, overhead light. It is a north light, which might be that of a painting from the nineteenth century, a light for which Seidner has a particular affinity.

12. The stage also comes to mind in connection with the women whom we see alone in hotel rooms, those ripely languorous models, with flowing hair, who recall – in some facial detail or in a pose, an accessory, an air – the Italy of Neo-Realist films, that flamboyant, cerebral world.

Finally, theatre is there in the omnipresent mirror, in reflection and relief, and in broken glass, with all its magical connotations, its heavy burden of myth: fairytale and Cocteau, Freud and Lacan, Venice and Narcissus, a flaw in the structure.... But we shall choose to regard it as one last manifestation of an idea that runs all through this work: the undermining of the sustaining illusion of identity. Identity like one of those sandbanks in the River Nile which are said to accumulate at random around some clump of reeds, creating an island where birds may nest and travellers halt, only to disappear without a trace, one day, from the surface of things.

PLATES

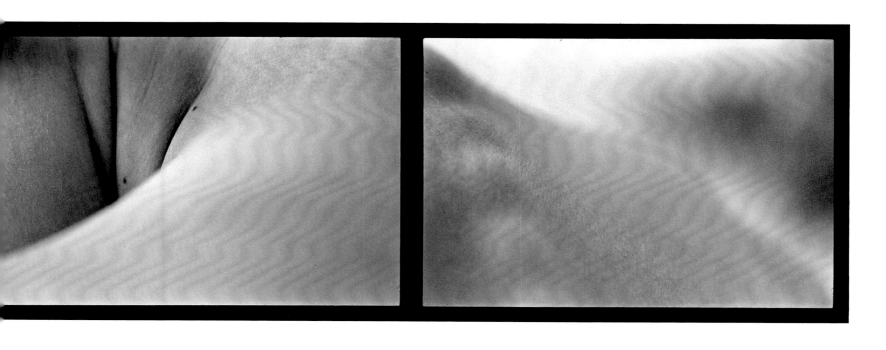

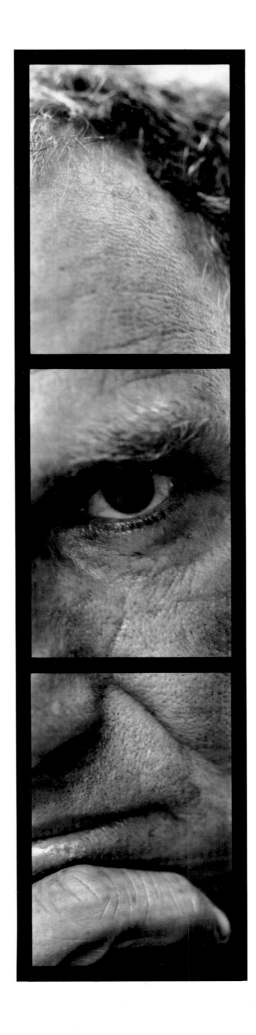

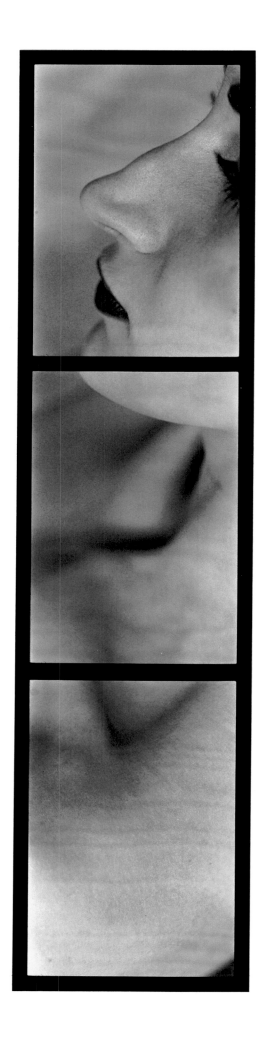

4

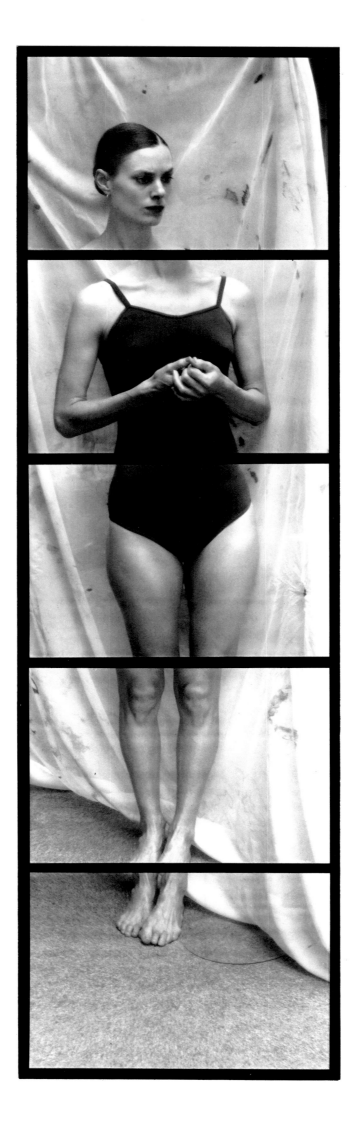

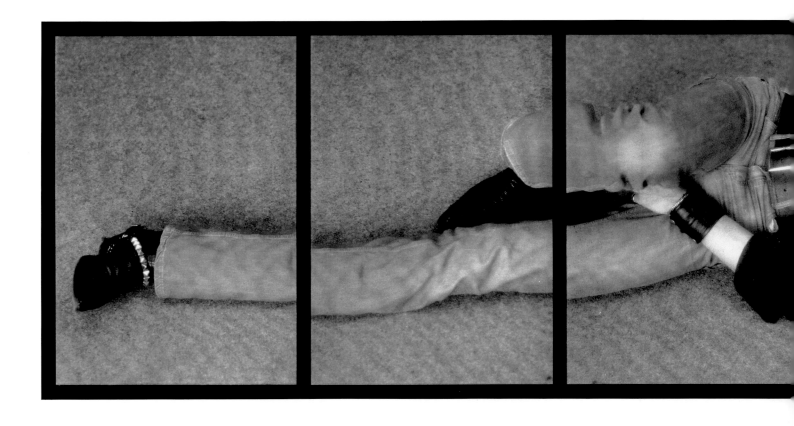

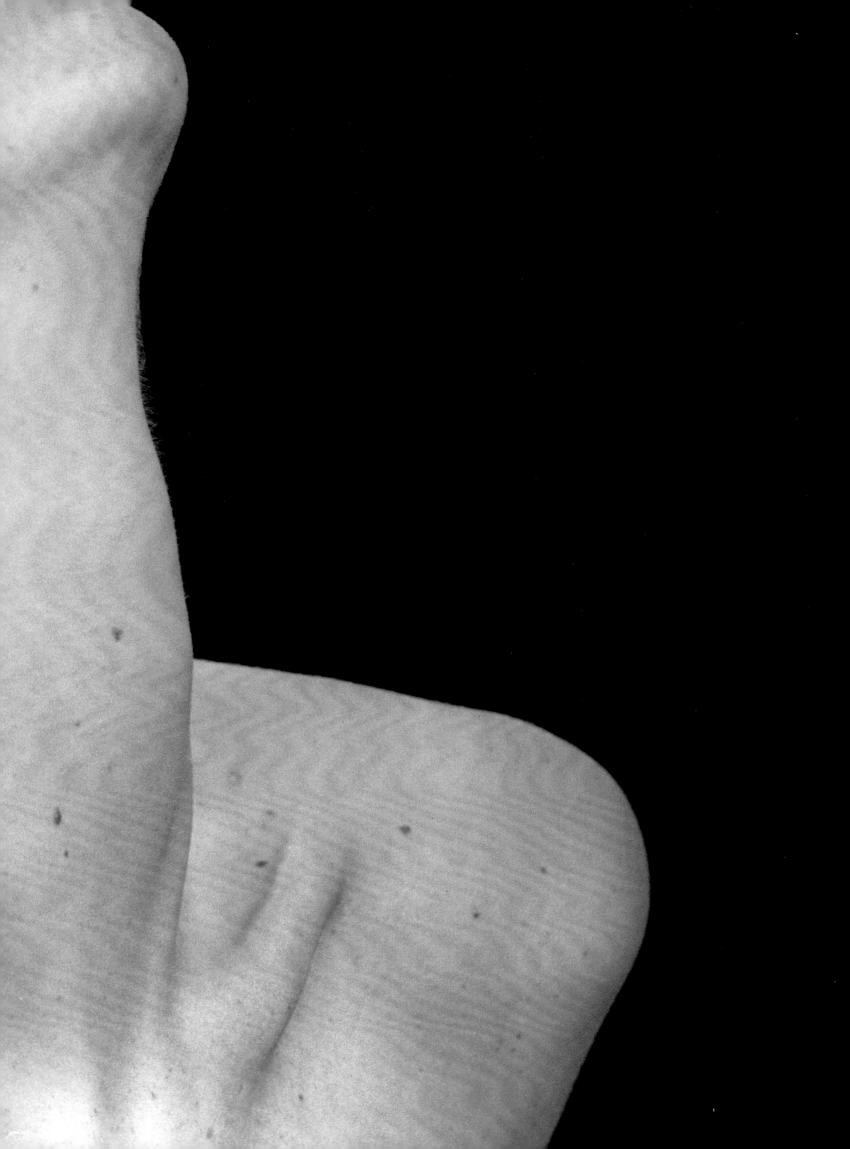

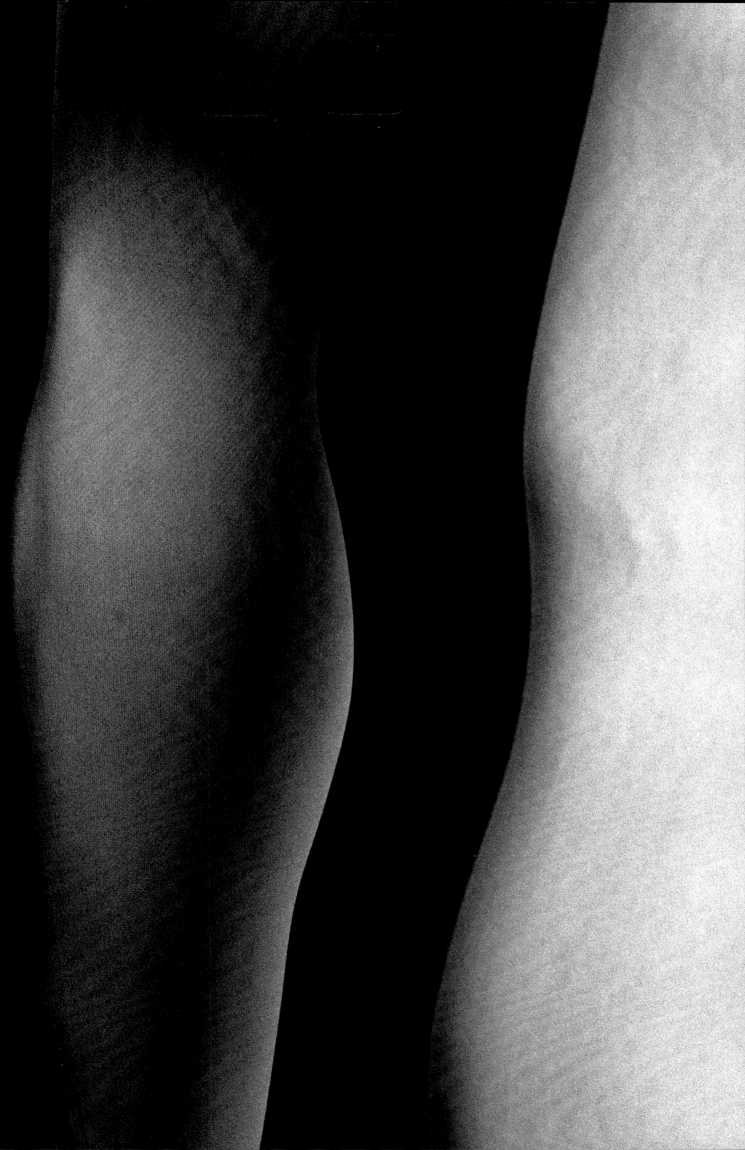

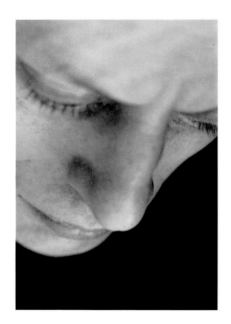

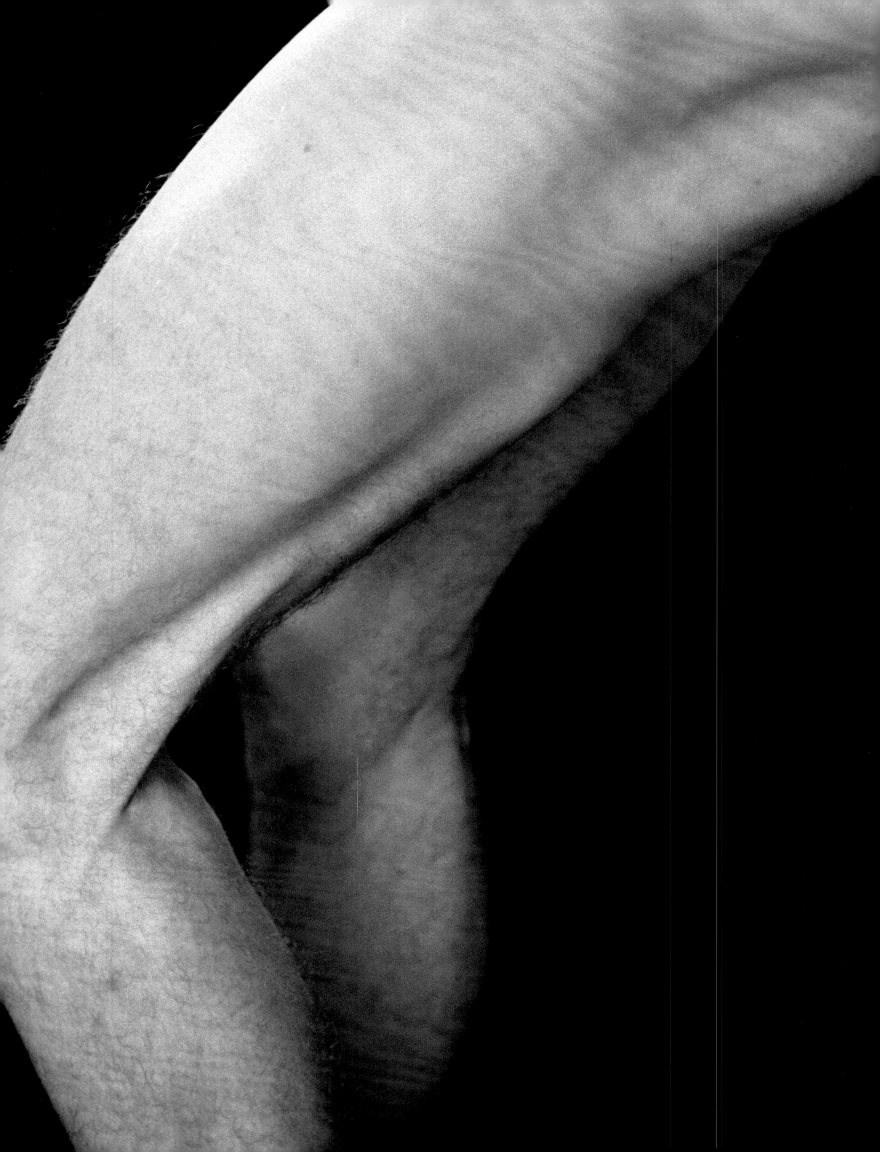

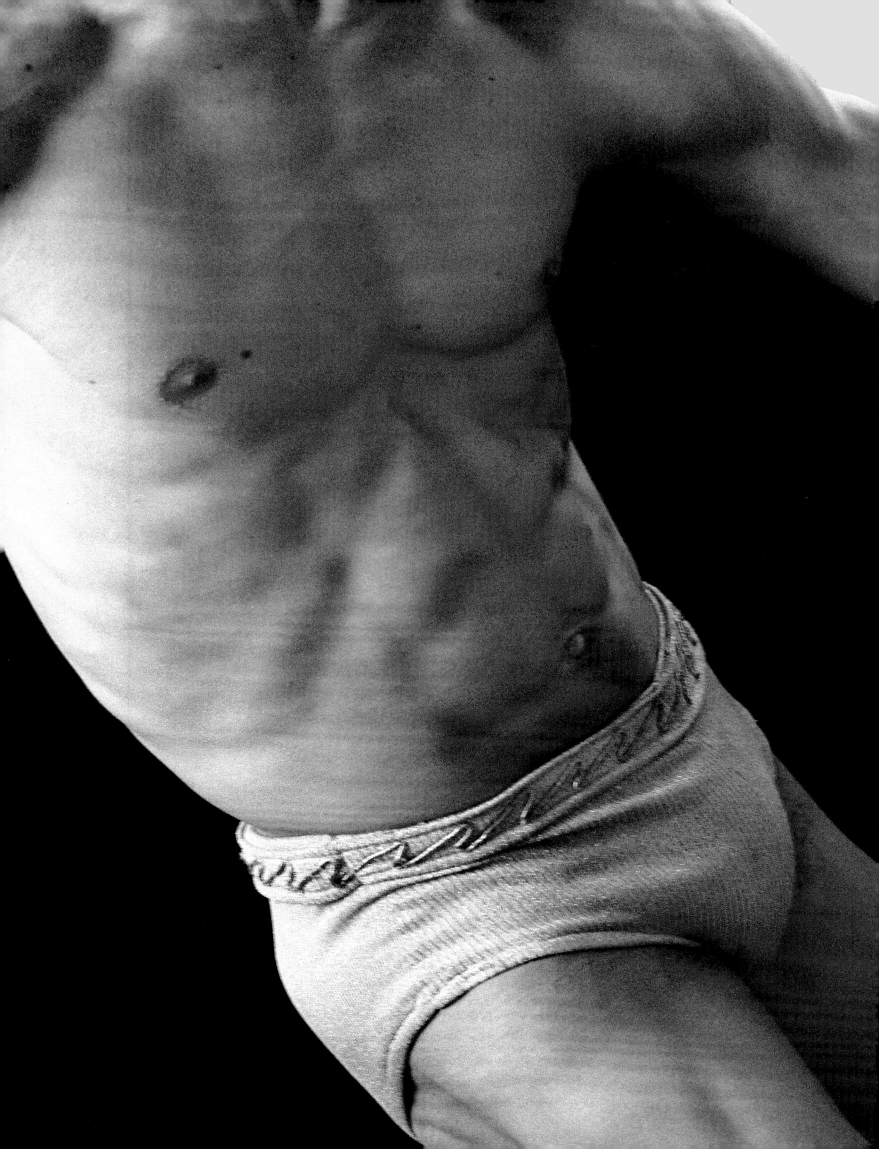

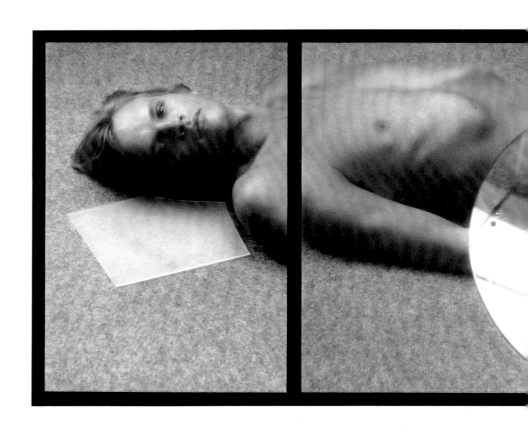

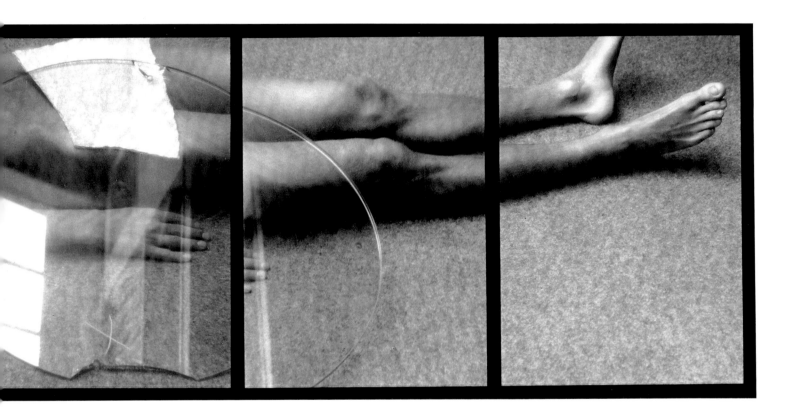

LIST OF PLATES

ADELLE LUTZ   1986

3

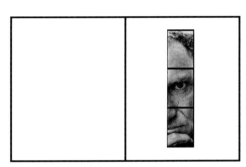

RICHARD SERRA   1980

1

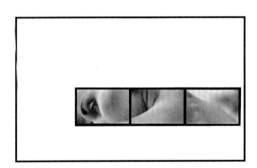

VIOLETA SANCHEZ   1979

4   5

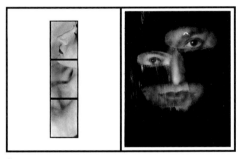

VIOLETA SANCHEZ   1979
UNTITLED   1986

2

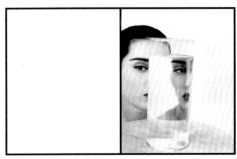

ROSIMA   1984

6   7

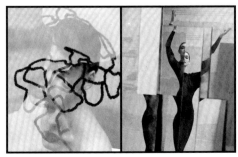

DANIELA STINEA, HAT BY
JACQUES LE CORRE, VOGUE BELLEZZA 1987
FRANCINE HOWELL, AZZEDINE ALAÏA 1986

8

LUCINDA CHILDS 1978

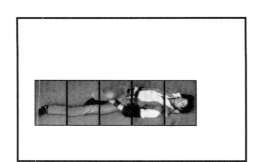

9

ROBERT MAPPLETHORPE 1978

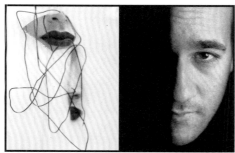

10

BETTY LAGO, AZZEDINE ALAÏA 1986

11 12

LIPS 1988
PATRICK MAURIÉS 1988

13 14

CARACAS-BALLET,
INTERVIEW MAGAZINE 1979

15 16

AHN DUONG, YVES SAINT LAURENT
HARPER'S & QUEEN 1986
DEBORAH KLEIN 1987

17

ANNE ROHART, YVES SAINT LAURENT 1983

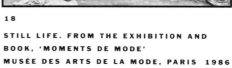

18

STILL LIFE. FROM THE EXHIBITION AND
BOOK, 'MOMENTS DE MODE'
MUSÉE DES ARTS DE LA MODE, PARIS 1986

19

SHELLEY DUVALL 1982

23

BRICE MARDEN 1987

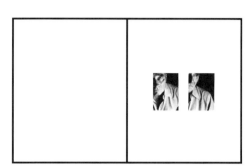

20

CHRISTOPHER ISHERWOOD 1979

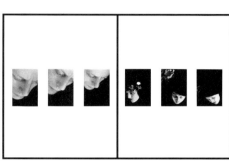

24 25

PHILIP GLASS 1979
SUZANNE HARRIS 1979

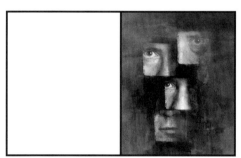

21

CHRISTIAN BOLTANSKI 1988

26 27

TAYA THURMAN, MME GRÈS 1980

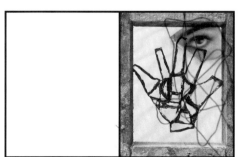

22

UNTITLED 1988

28

CINDY SHERMAN 1984

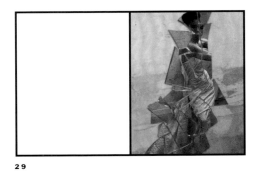

29

FRANCINE HOWELL, VICTOR EDELSTEIN
HARPER'S & QUEEN   1987

34

BETTY LAGO, UNGARO
INTERVIEW MAGAZINE   1985

30   31

ALBERTO MORAVIA, MAX MAGAZINE   1989
VALENTINO, ITALIAN VOGUE   1984

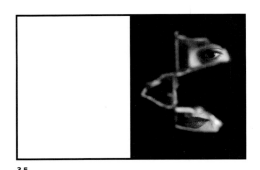

35

CAROLINE ELLEN, ITALIAN VOGUE   1987

32

DANIELA STINEA   1987

36

FRANCINE HOWELL, AZZEDINE ALAÏA   1986

33

ELÉONORE LE MONNIER   1986

37

CYNTHIA ANTHONIO, PATOU
ITALIAN VOGUE   1987

38

'ROBES VOLANTES'.
FROM THE EXHIBITION AND
BOOK, 'MOMENTS DE MODE'
MUSÉE DES ARTS DE LA MODE, PARIS 1986

42

ANNE ROHART, YVES SAINT LAURENT 1983

39

EVENING GOWN BY WORTH.
FROM THE EXHIBITION AND
BOOK, 'MOMENTS DE MODE'
MUSÉE DES ARTS DE LA MODE, PARIS 1986

43

PALOMA PICASSO, JARDIN DES MODES 1987

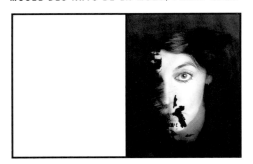

40

ANETTE MESSAGER   1988

44   45

DRAGANA KUNJADIC, ITALIAN VOGUE   1988
BANDAGES   1982

41

SIMONETTA GIANFELICI, VALENTINO
ITALIAN VOGUE   1984

46

ROSIMA, ITALIAN VOGUE   1986

47   48

TINA CHOW   1979

49   50

ADELLE LUTZ   1986

FRANCINE HOWELL   1986

51   52

HECTOR OREZZOLI   1987

MARCIAL BERRO   1980

53

SELF-PORTRAIT   1989

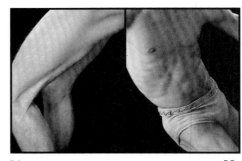

54   55

CARACAS-BALLET

INTERVIEW MAGAZINE   1979

56

CAROLINE ELLEN   1985

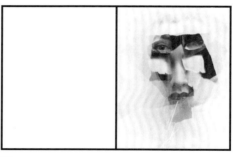

57

FRANCINE HOWELL, ITALIAN VOGUE   1987

58   59

DAVID BYRNE   1982

60/61

PRUDENCE WALTERS
HOMAGE TO BLUMENFELD   1984

67

'ROBE À LA FRANÇAISE'.
FROM THE EXHIBITION AND
BOOK, 'MOMENTS DE MODE'
MUSÉE DES ARTS DE LA MODE, PARIS 1986

62   63

JENE HIGHSTEIN   1979
CHARLES MOULTON   1980

68

THÉRÈSE BACHY, FRENCH VOGUE   1987

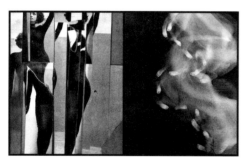

64   65

BETTY LAGO, AZZEDINE ALAÏA   1986
FEET   1987

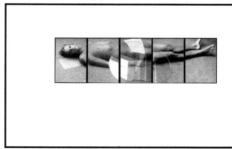

69

JENS LIPP   1978

66

HAT BY BALENCIAGA   1988

70

CELINA FISCHER VON CZETTRITZ   1988

DAVID SEIDNER   **BORN IN LOS ANGELES 1957**

SOLO EXHIBITIONS

1989 SAMIA SAOUMA GALLERY   PARIS
1986 MUSÉE DES ARTS DE LA MODE   PARIS
1985 SAMIA SAOUMA GALLERY   PARIS
1983 LA REMISE DU PARC   PARIS
1982 TON PEEK GALLERY   UTRECHT
1982 ERHARDT GALLERY   NUREMBERG
1982 UGO FERRANTI GALLERY   ROME
1981 THE CLOCK TOWER   NEW YORK
1980 LA REMISE DU PARC   PARIS
1979 LOS ANGELES INSTITUTE OF CONTEMPORARY ART   LOS ANGELES
1978 LA REMISE DU PARC   PARIS

GROUP EXHIBITIONS

1989 YVES SAINT LAURENT — PHOTOGRAPHIES DE MODE, CENTRE POMPIDOU   PARIS
1988 CRÉATEURS DE MODE, CRÉATEURS D'IMAGE. MUSÉE DES ARTS DÉCORATIFS   PARIS
1987 THE SPIRAL OF CREATIVITY. HALL WALLS, BUFFALO   NEW YORK
1986 PUBLIC — PRIVATE. MUSEUM OF CONTEMPORARY PHOTOGRAPHY   CHICAGO
1984 20 ANNI DI VOGUE. SAGRATO DUOMO   MILAN
1982 FACES PHOTOGRAPHED. GREY ART GALLERY   NEW YORK UNIVERSITY
1982 MODERN MASTERS. GOVINDA GALLERY   WASHINGTON D.C.
1980 AUTOPORTRAITS. LA REMISE DU PARC   PARIS
1979 ARTISTS BY ARTISTS. WHITNEY MUSEUM, DOWNTOWN BRANCH   NEW YORK

PUBLICATIONS

NO. 2 LES CAHIERS DE L'ENERGUMÈNE   PARIS 1983
MOMENTS DE MODE. EDITIONS HERSCHER   PARIS 1986
DAVID SEIDNER, PHOTOGRAPHIEN. SCHIRMER/MOSEL   MUNICH 1989

CONTRIBUTING EDITOR TO BOMB MAGAZINE

PHOTOGRAPHS APPEAR REGULARLY IN ITALIAN VOGUE AND HARPER'S & QUEEN